HIP HOP
Coloring and Activity Book

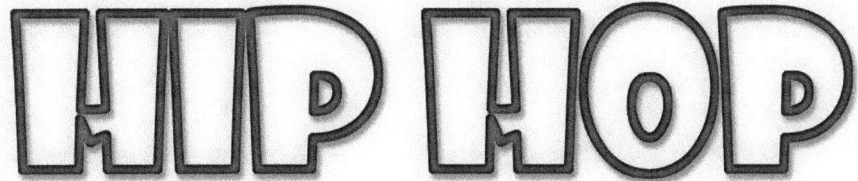

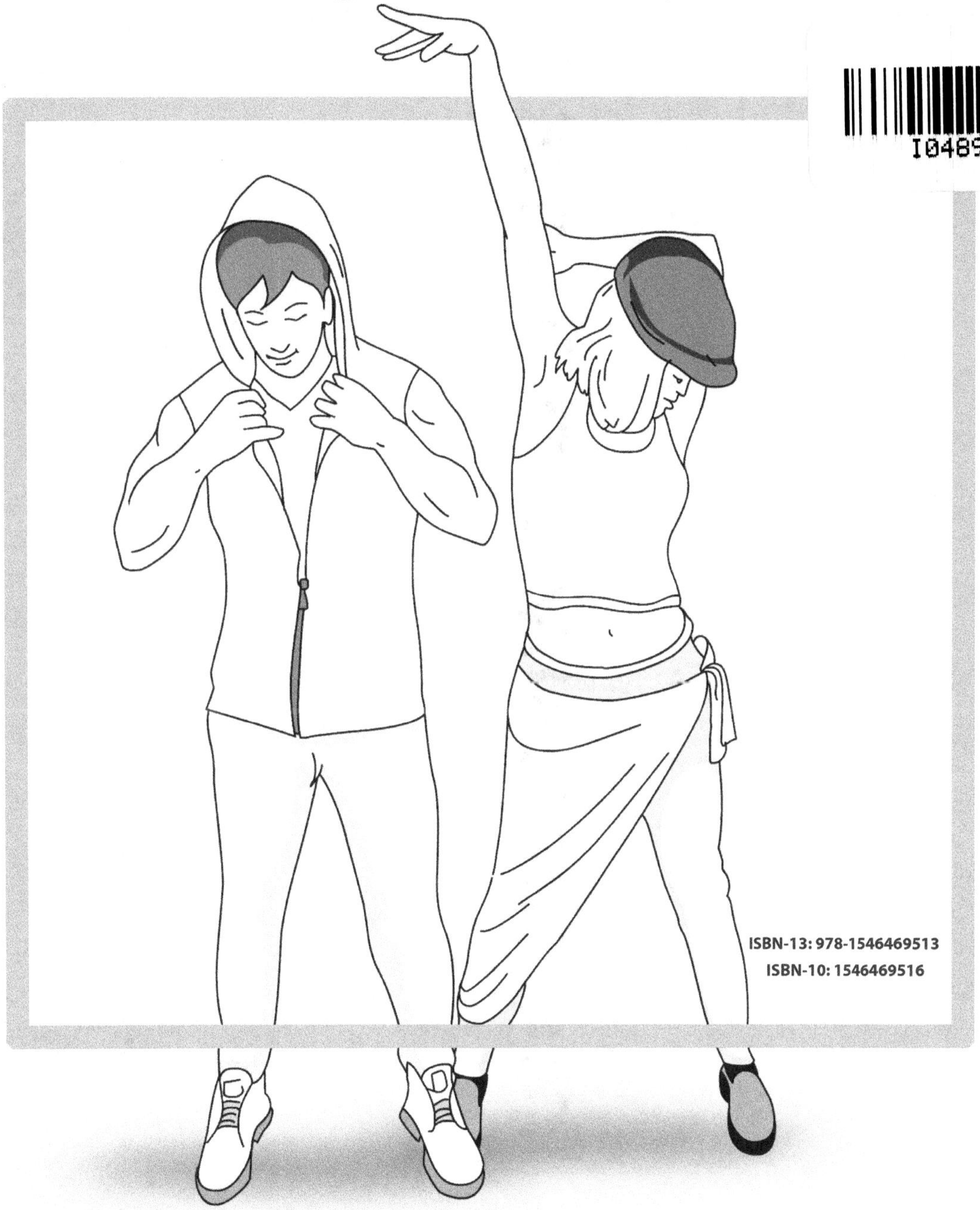

ISBN-13: 978-1546469513

ISBN-10: 1546469516

Copyright © 2017 by Idan Boaz

Intentionally Left Blank

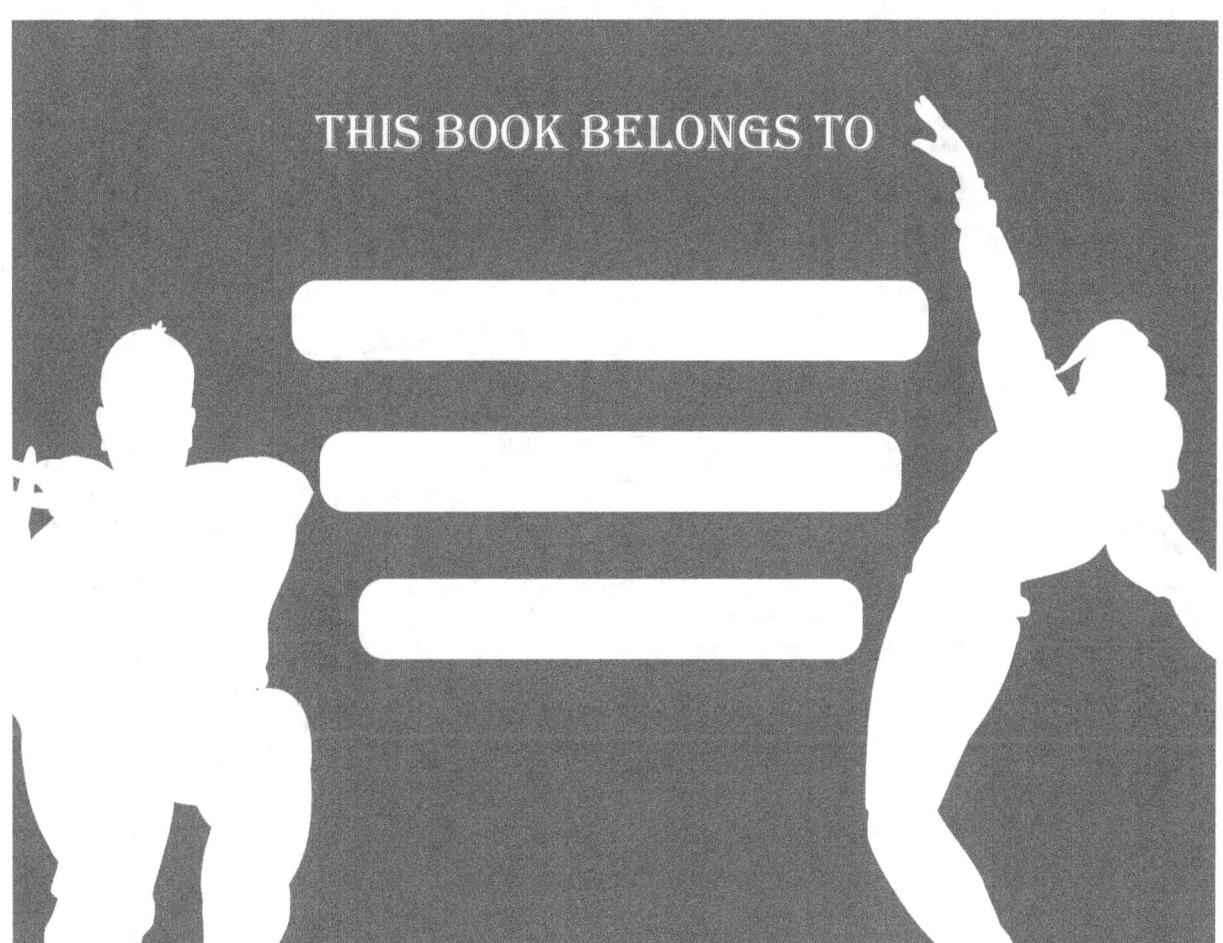

THIS BOOK BELONGS TO

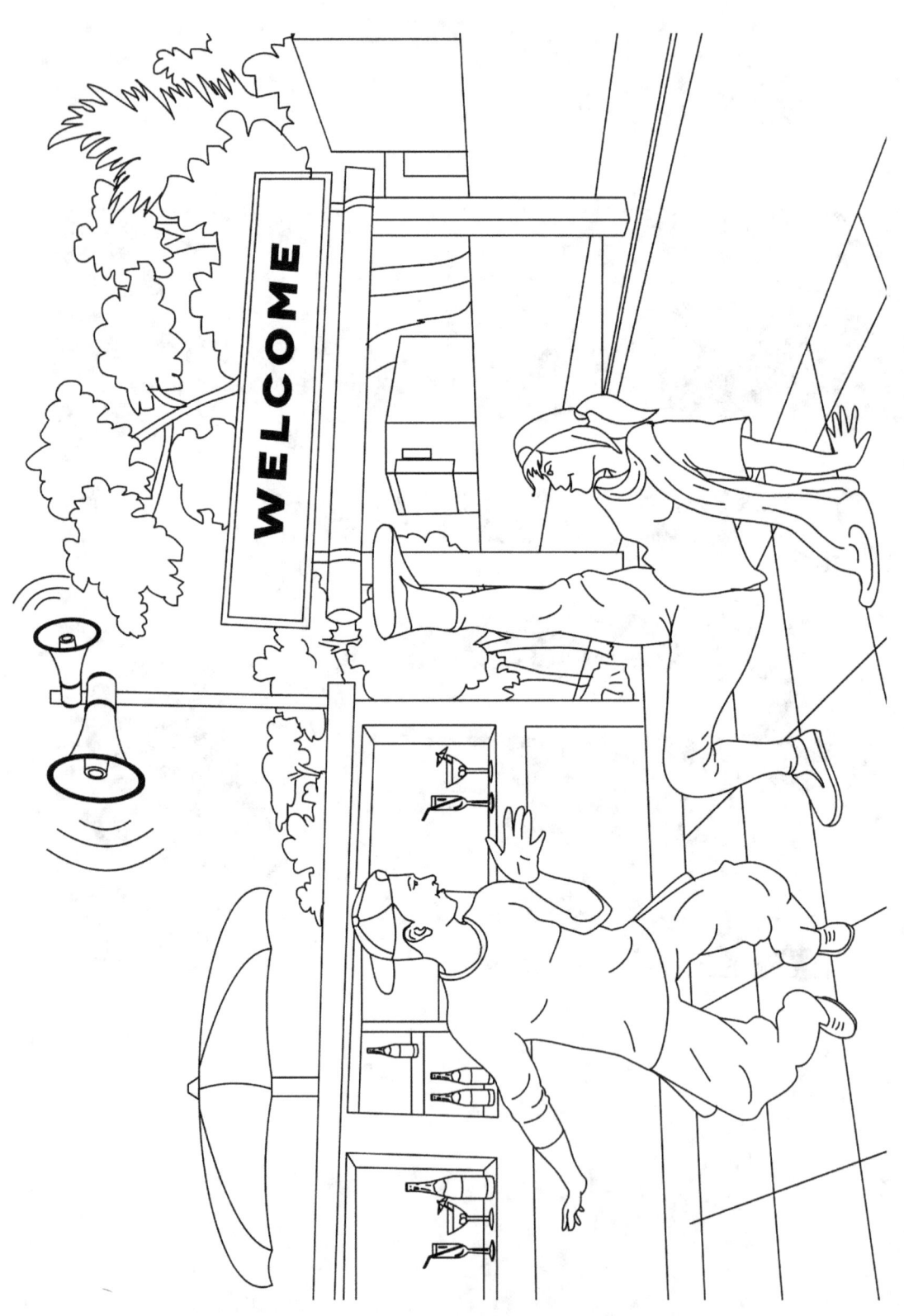

Hip Hop is feeling the music and dancing to the beat, The fun dance step here is actually "Happy Feet". What is Hip Hop? It is the dance that you will surely love the most, Color this page first before you do the "Criss Cross".

You can dance Hip Hop everywhere, it's really FUN! It's cool to dance with your friends even under the sun. Best way to learn is try out new moves, like the one they call "Gliding", It's quite simple just like coloring this page, which surely you'll be enjoying.

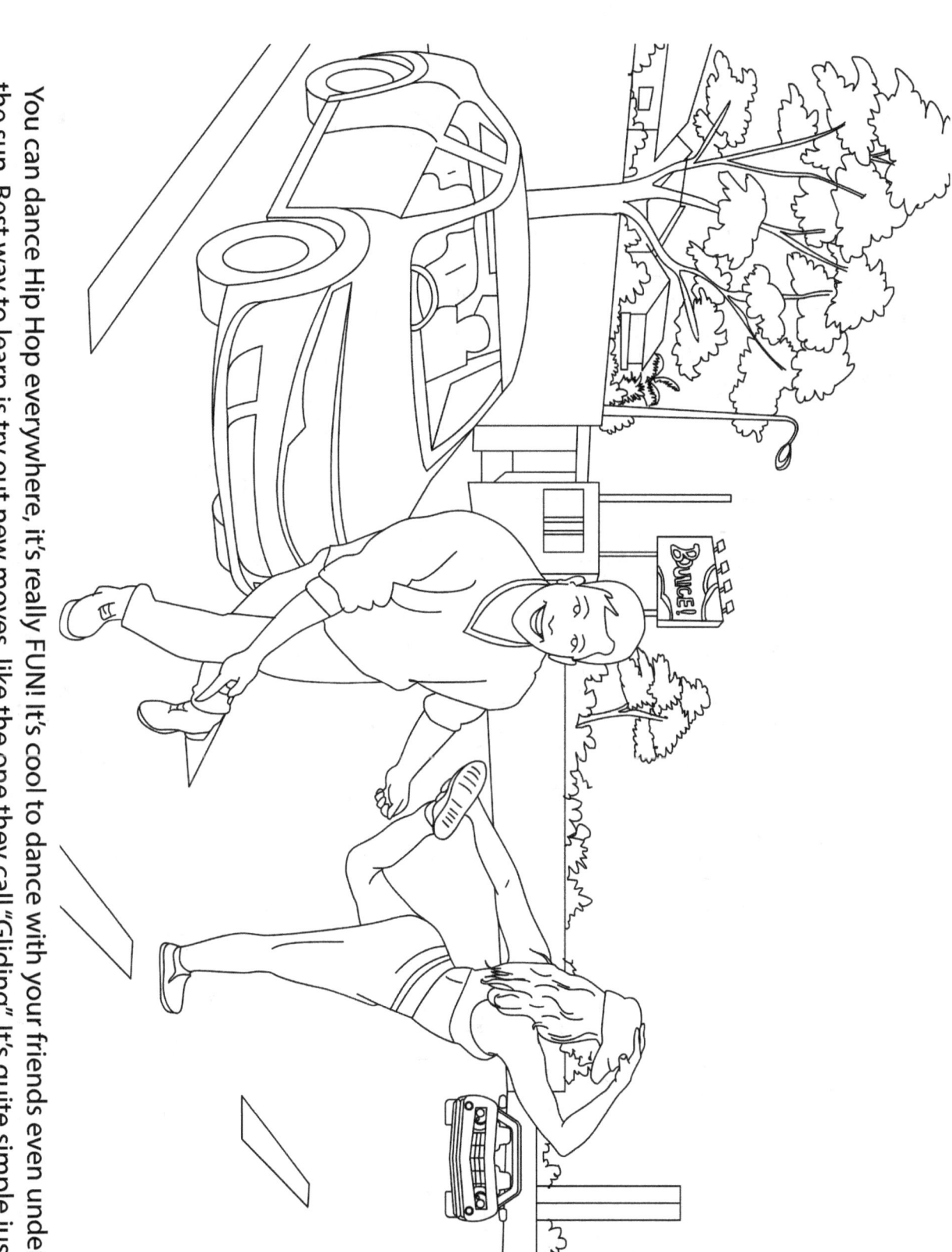

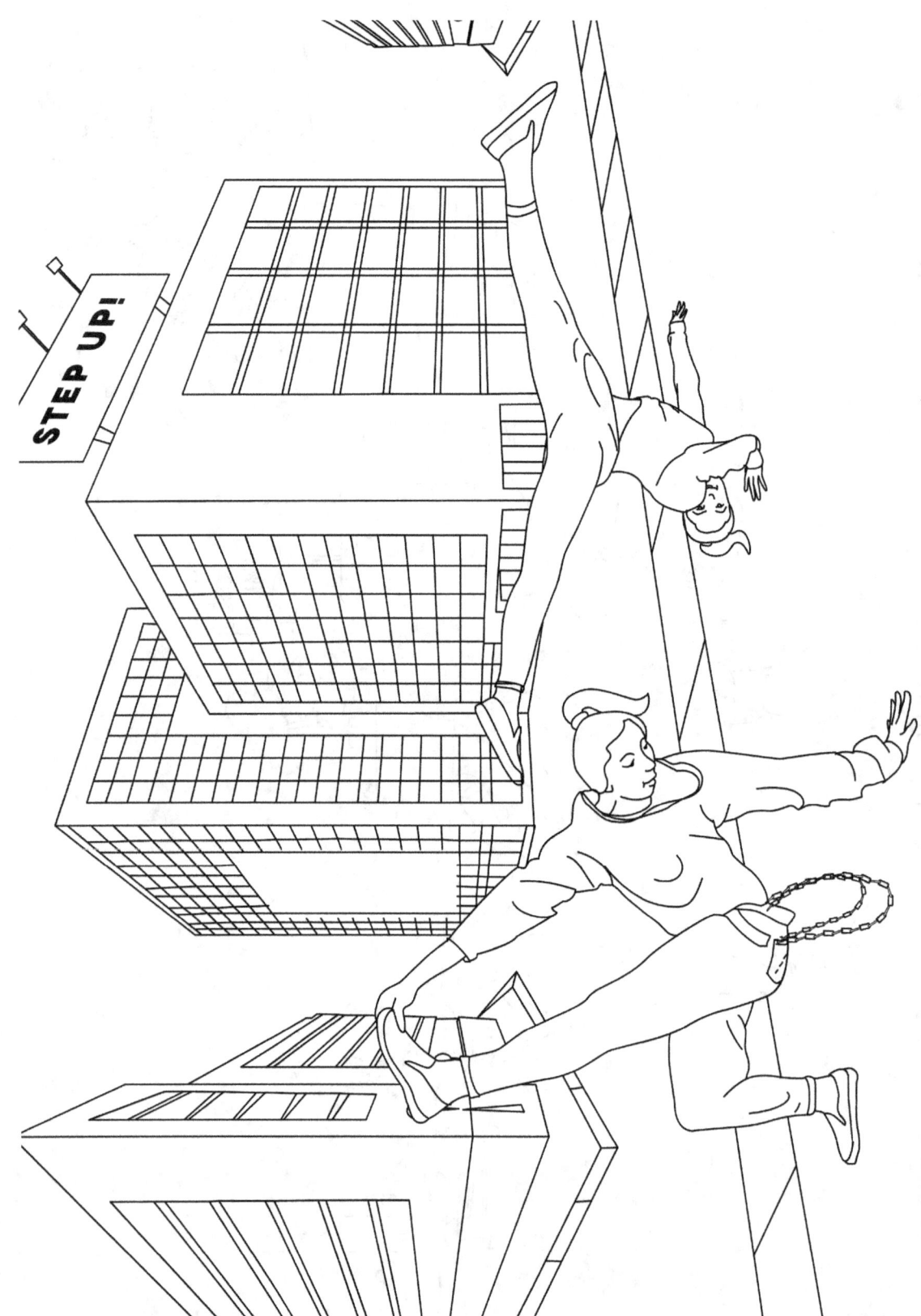

"Breaking" is another fun Hip Hop move, When there's good music, you can really groove. You may be stiff at first try but you can work on your vibe, Now, try to color the buildings with colors that jive.

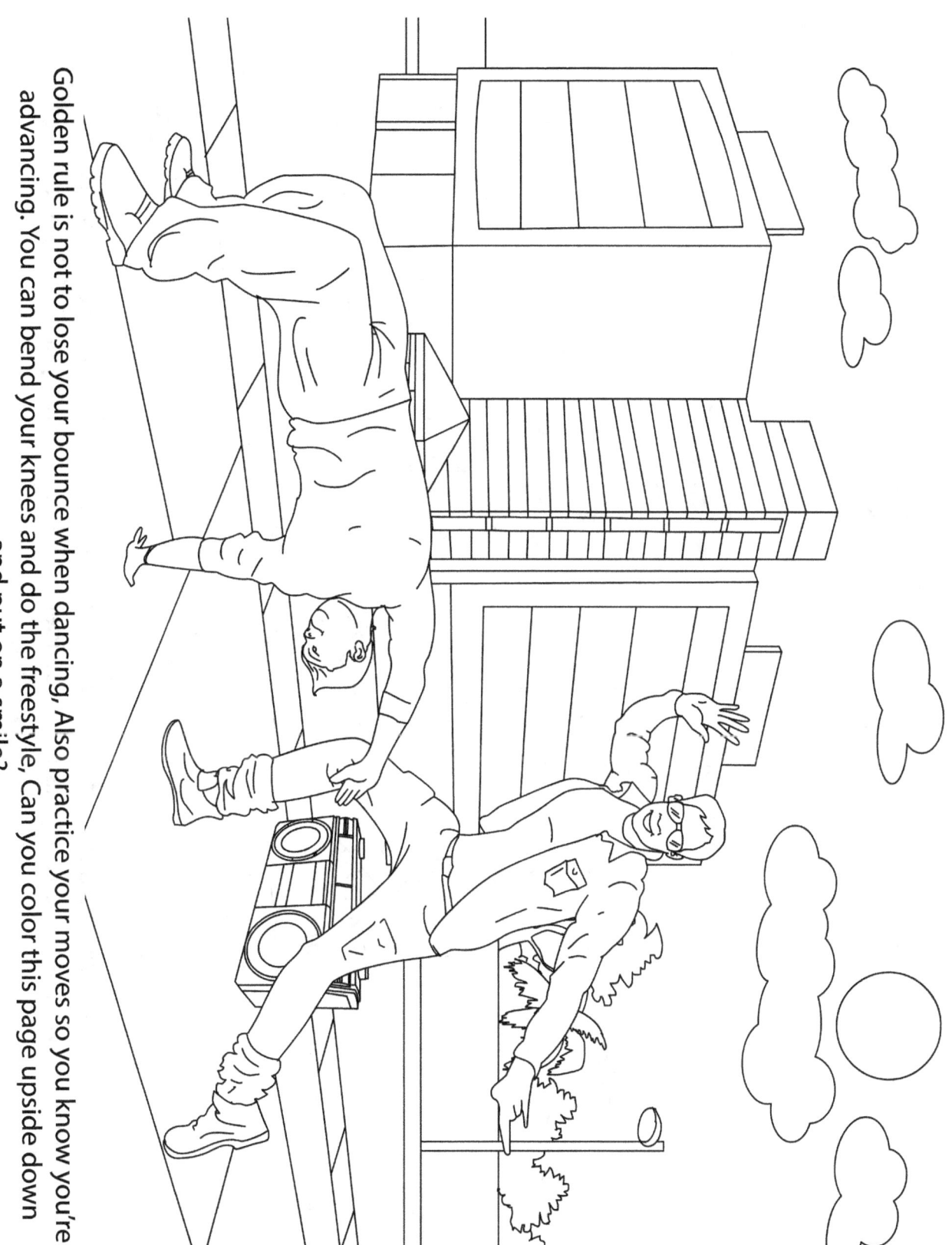

Golden rule is not to lose your bounce when dancing. Also practice your moves so you know you're advancing. You can bend your knees and do the freestyle. Can you color this page upside down and put on a smile?

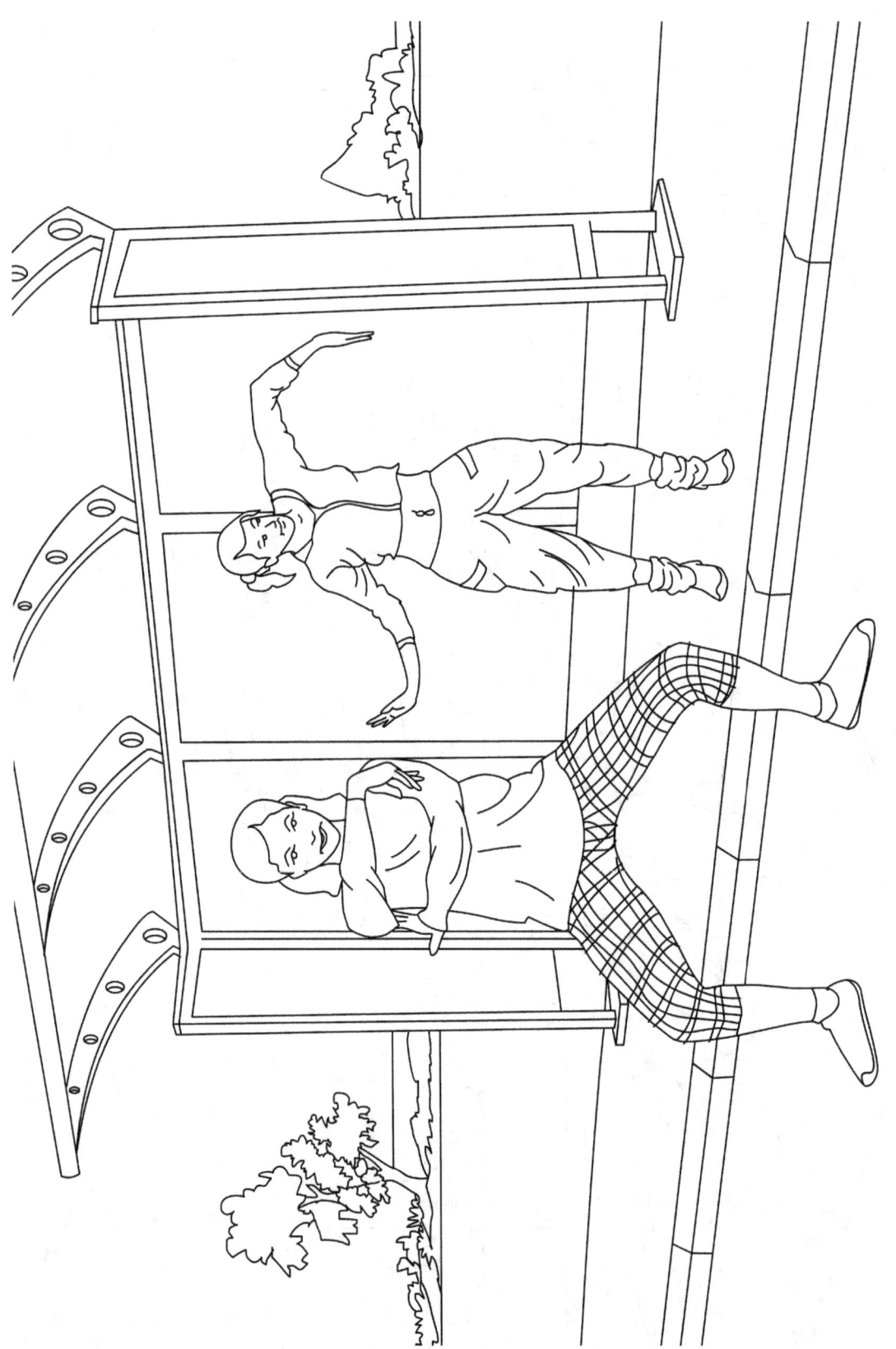

As a beginner, you should practice and do the "Arm Wave" wherever you are, With different hand movement techniques, you can go far! Can you identify where this fun place is? Try to color the whole picture fully without a miss.

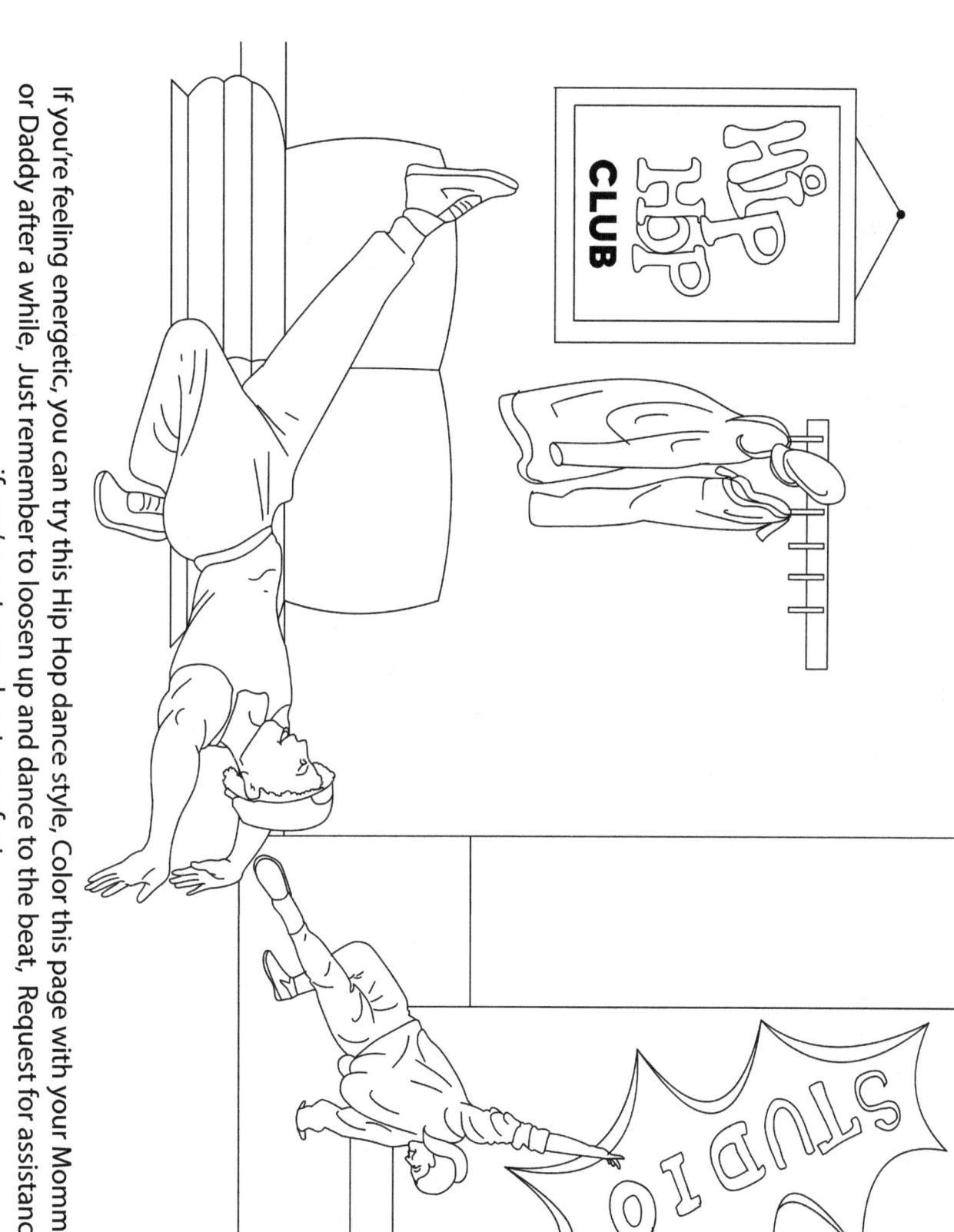

If you're feeling energetic, you can try this Hip Hop dance style. Color this page with your Mommy or Daddy after a while. Just remember to loosen up and dance to the beat. Request for assistance if you're not sure about your feet.

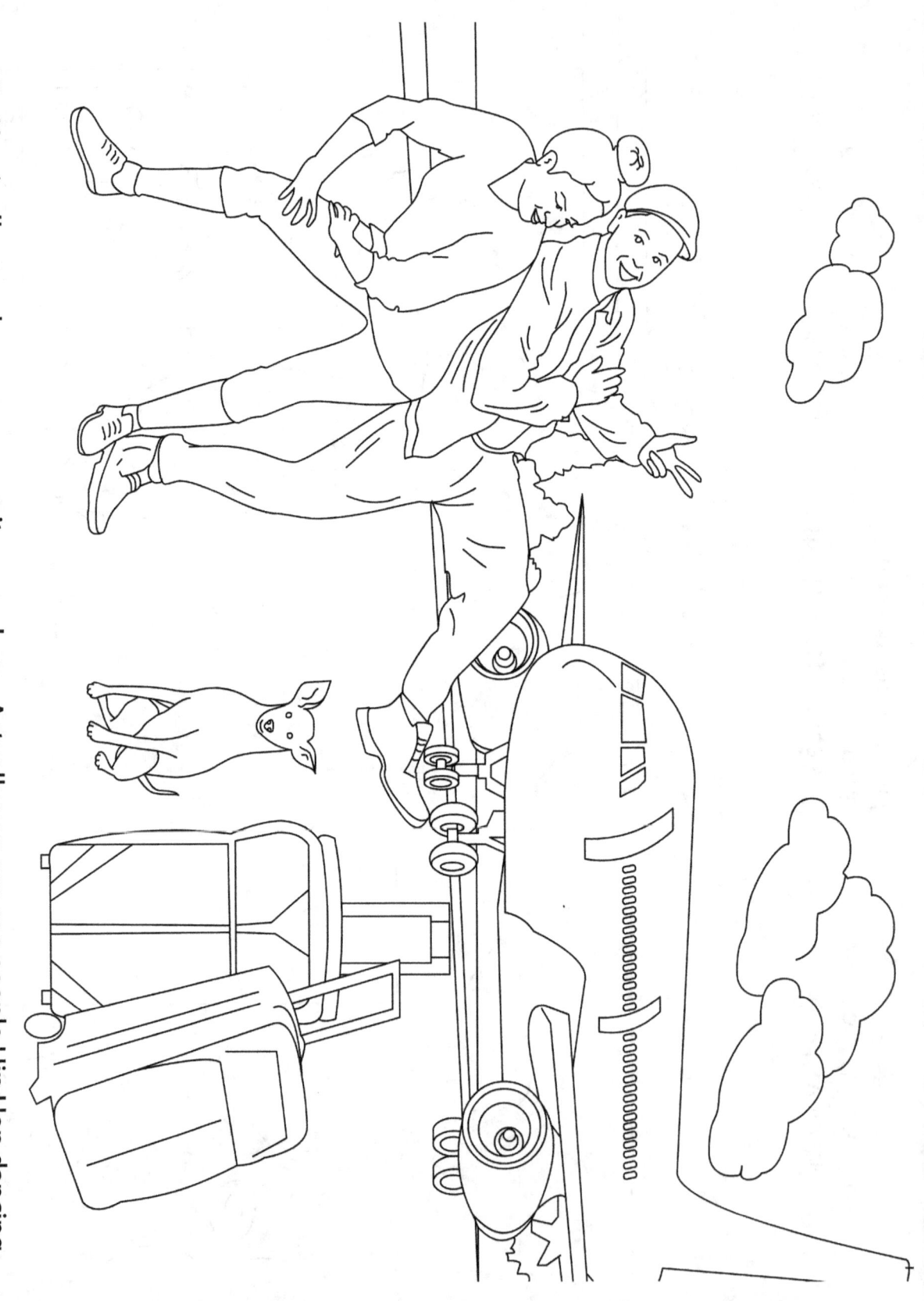

Hip Hop is all around us, you can see it everywhere. Actually you can see people Hip Hop dancing anywhere. Can you see the airplane at the back, is it already up in the air? Try to dance and color this page while sitting in a chair.

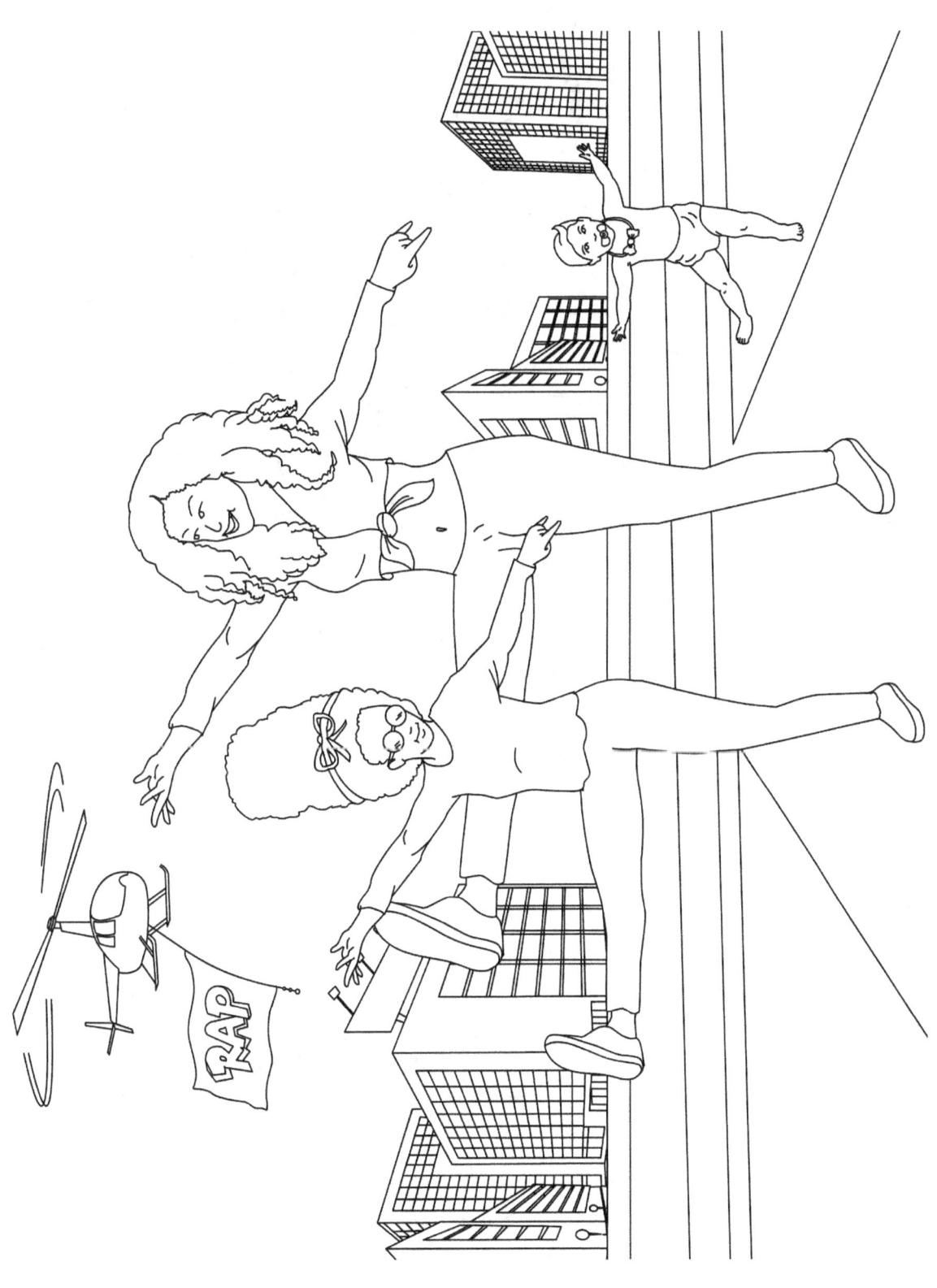

It's fun playing in the playground with your friends all day, You can also do the Hip Hop "Roll" and also the sway. Extend your legs, speed it up and throw your arms, Then color this page cheerfully and full of charms.

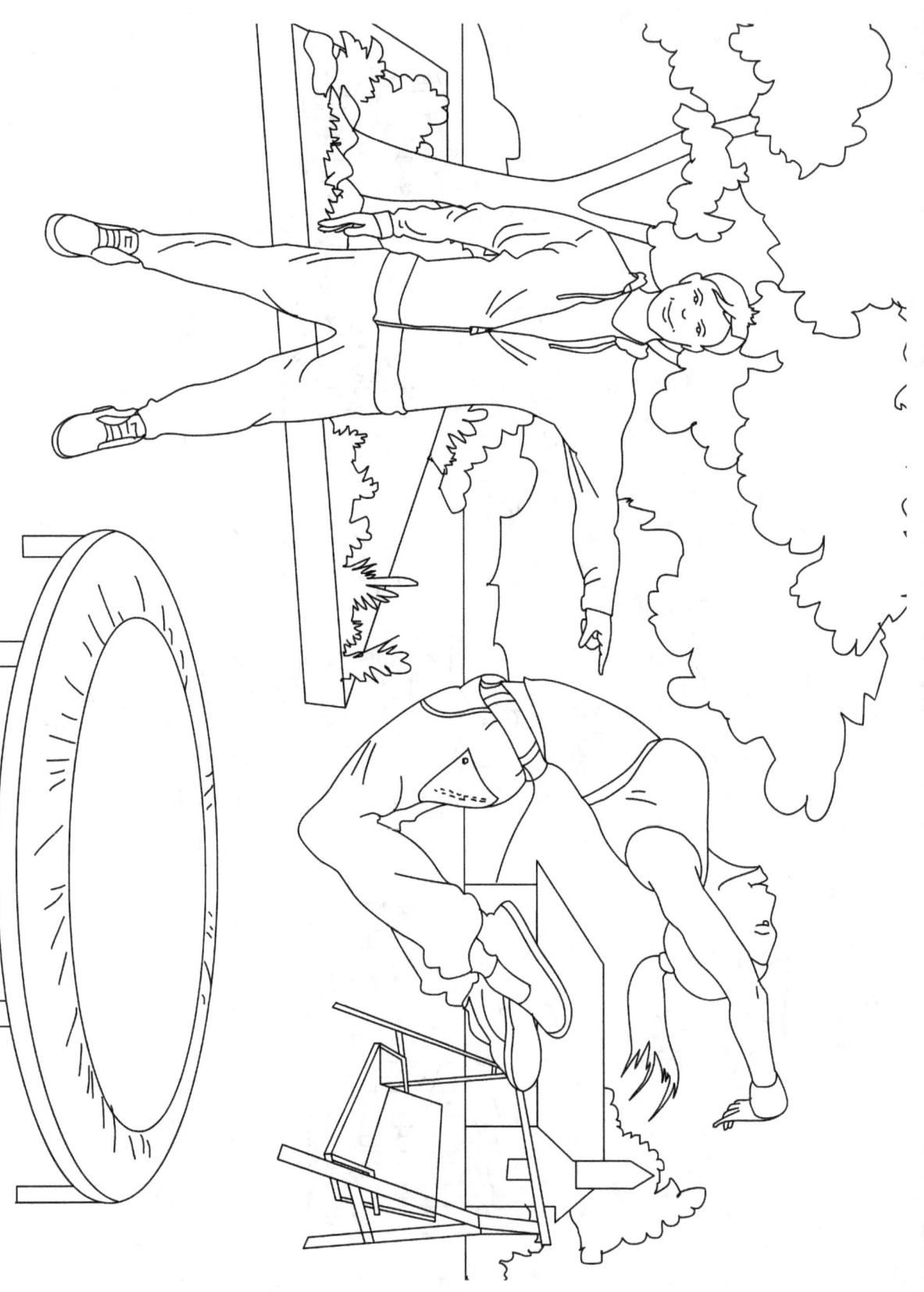

Jump, arc your body and just be free, Let go and dance the Hip Hop with all your glee.
Now color the stairs with different colors fast, Move quick, finishing this page is a must.

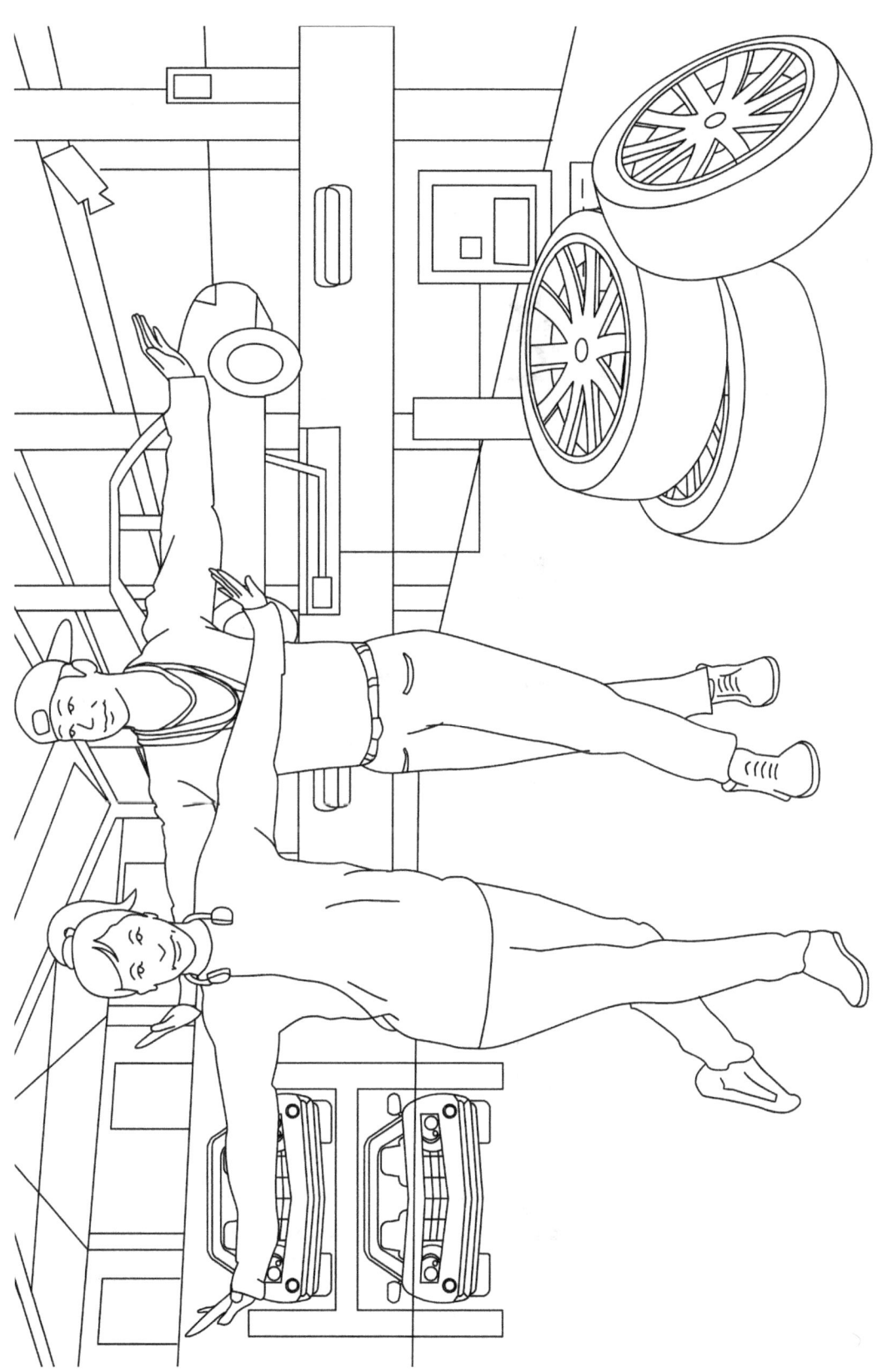

Do the Hip Hop "Arm Wave", do you remember how? Time to use your fingers, knuckles, wrist, elbow and shoulder now. How many cars can you spot in at the back?

Intentionally Left Blank

HIP HOP

Coloring and Activity Book

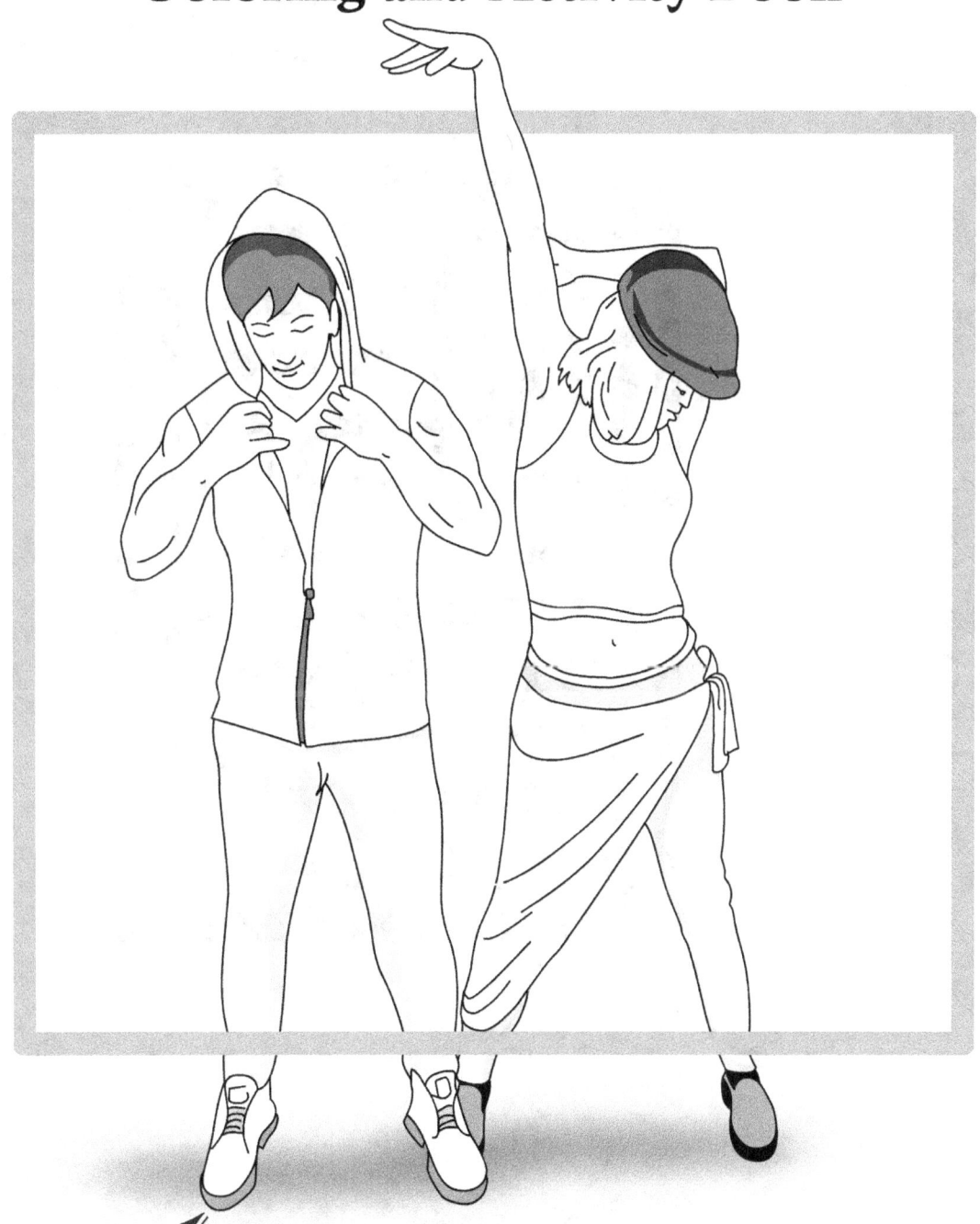

WORKSHEETS

Clap to keep with the beat, arms go out and do steps one and two, Time for some activity, this is a maze, you must find your way through. Now bend your knees, bounce and add a little flavor, It's simple, loosen your arms and do something major.

Last step, bend then put your arms in the air, only one at a time, Find your way through the maze, think clearly to save time. Finally, do the "Punch Down" and move side to side,

Are you happy? You now know Hip Hop, smile!

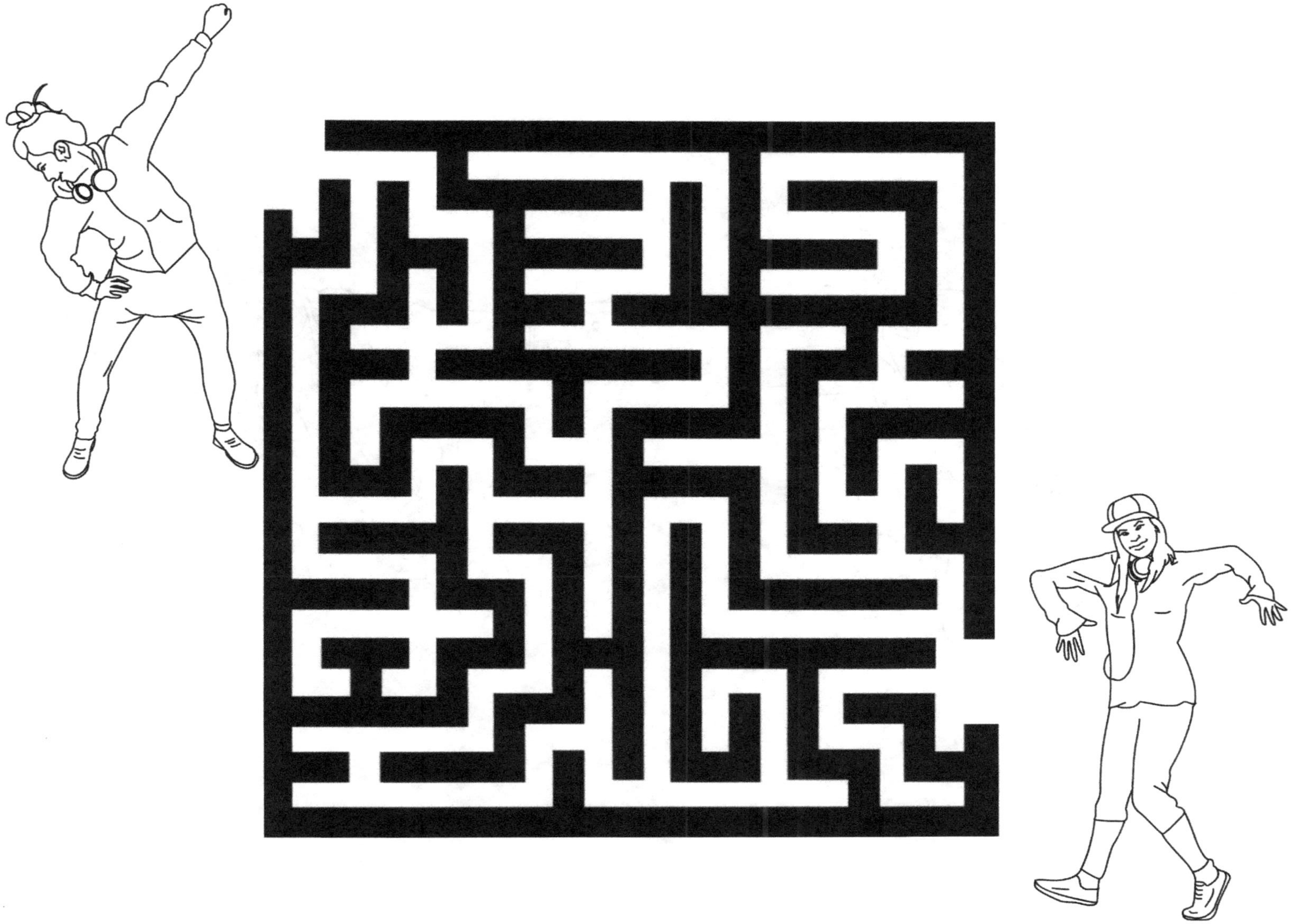

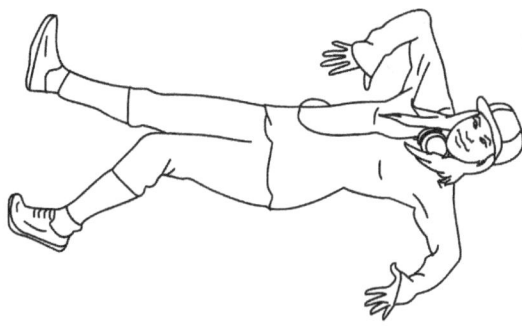

Spot 4 Differences

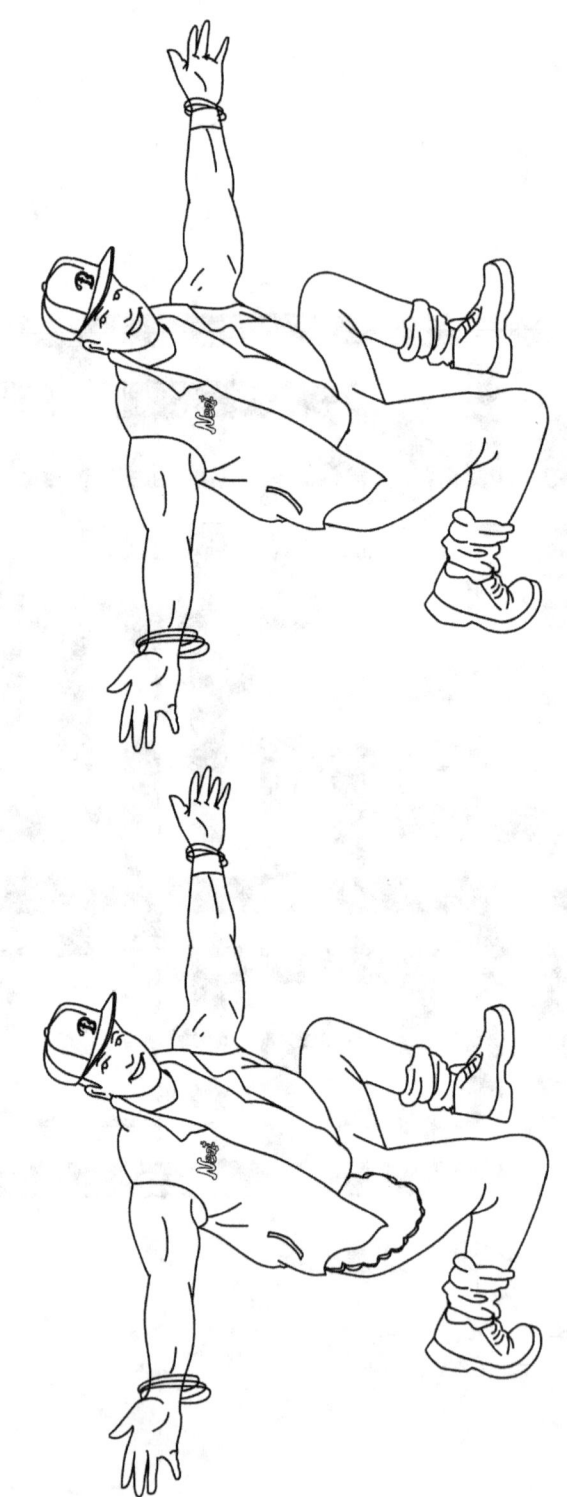

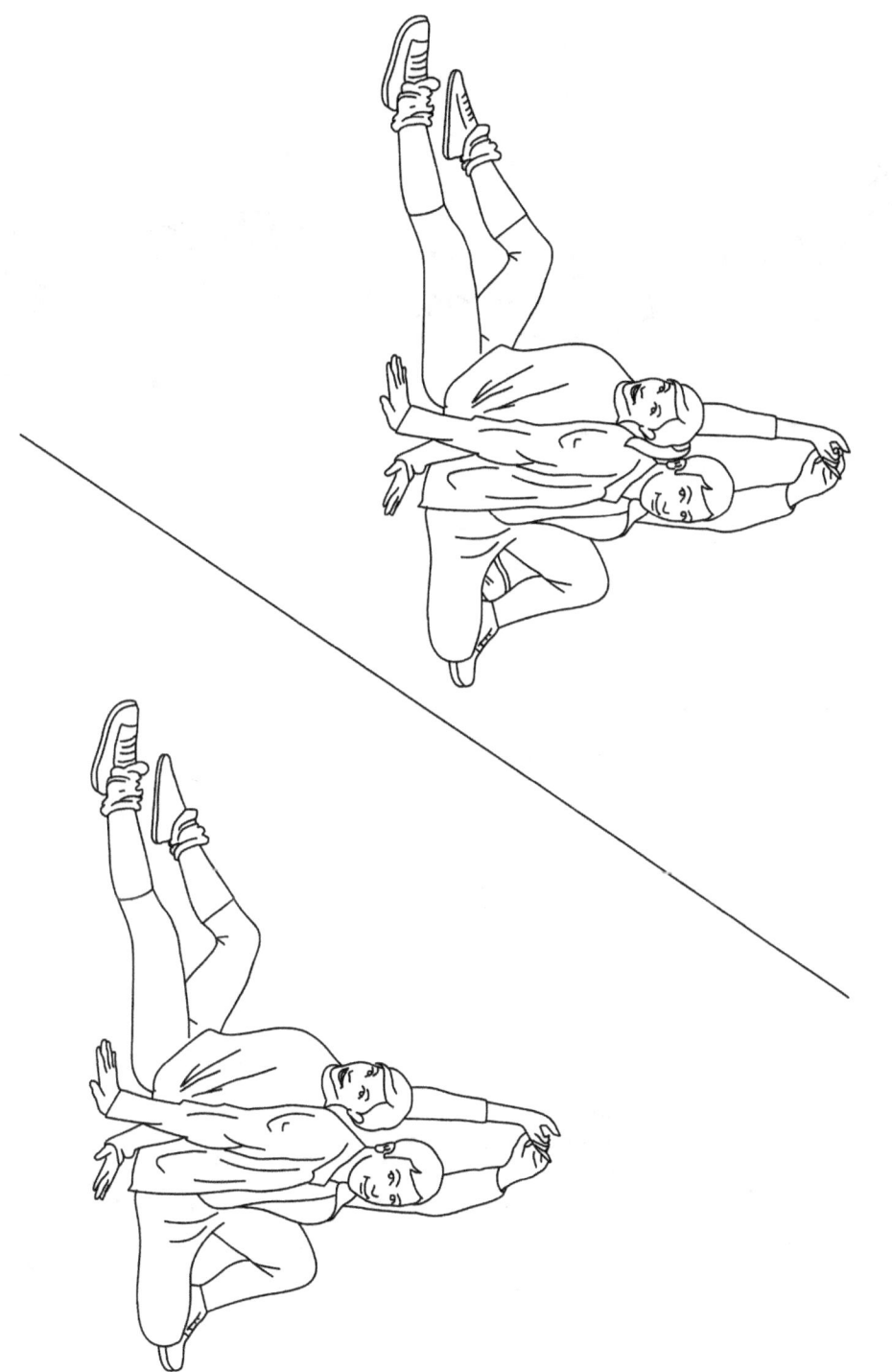

Spot 4 Differences

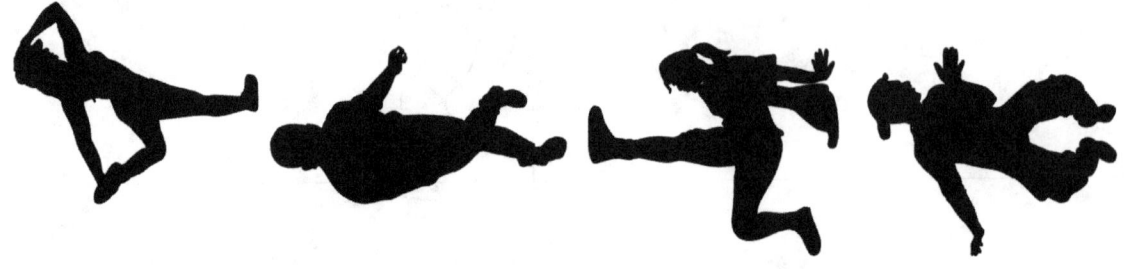

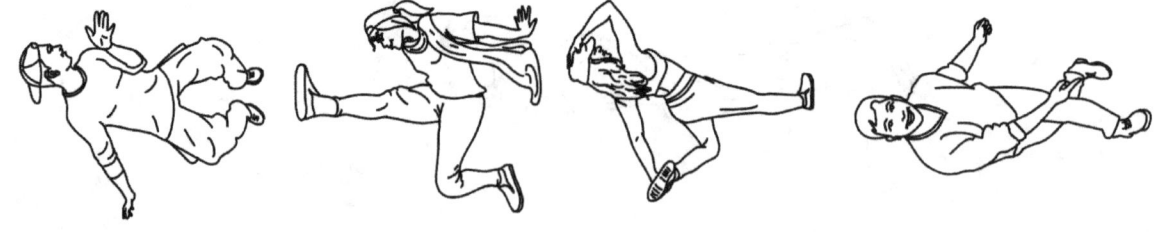

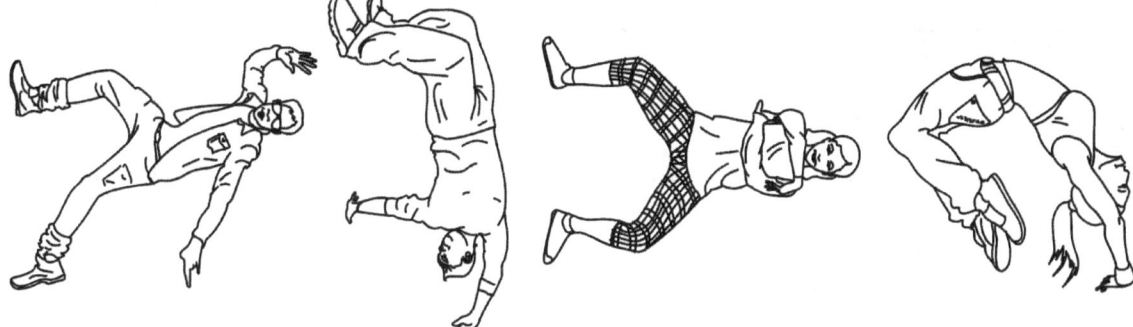

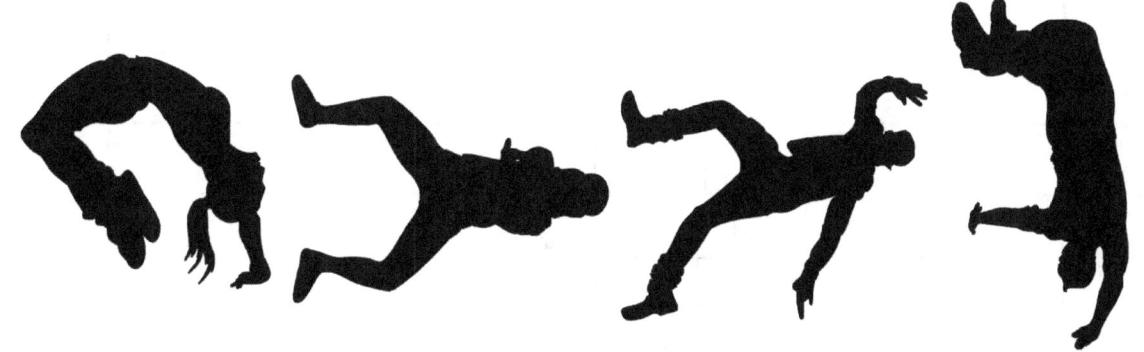

Copy the Picture

Copy the picture using the grid lines as a guide
you might find it easier to copy one square at a time

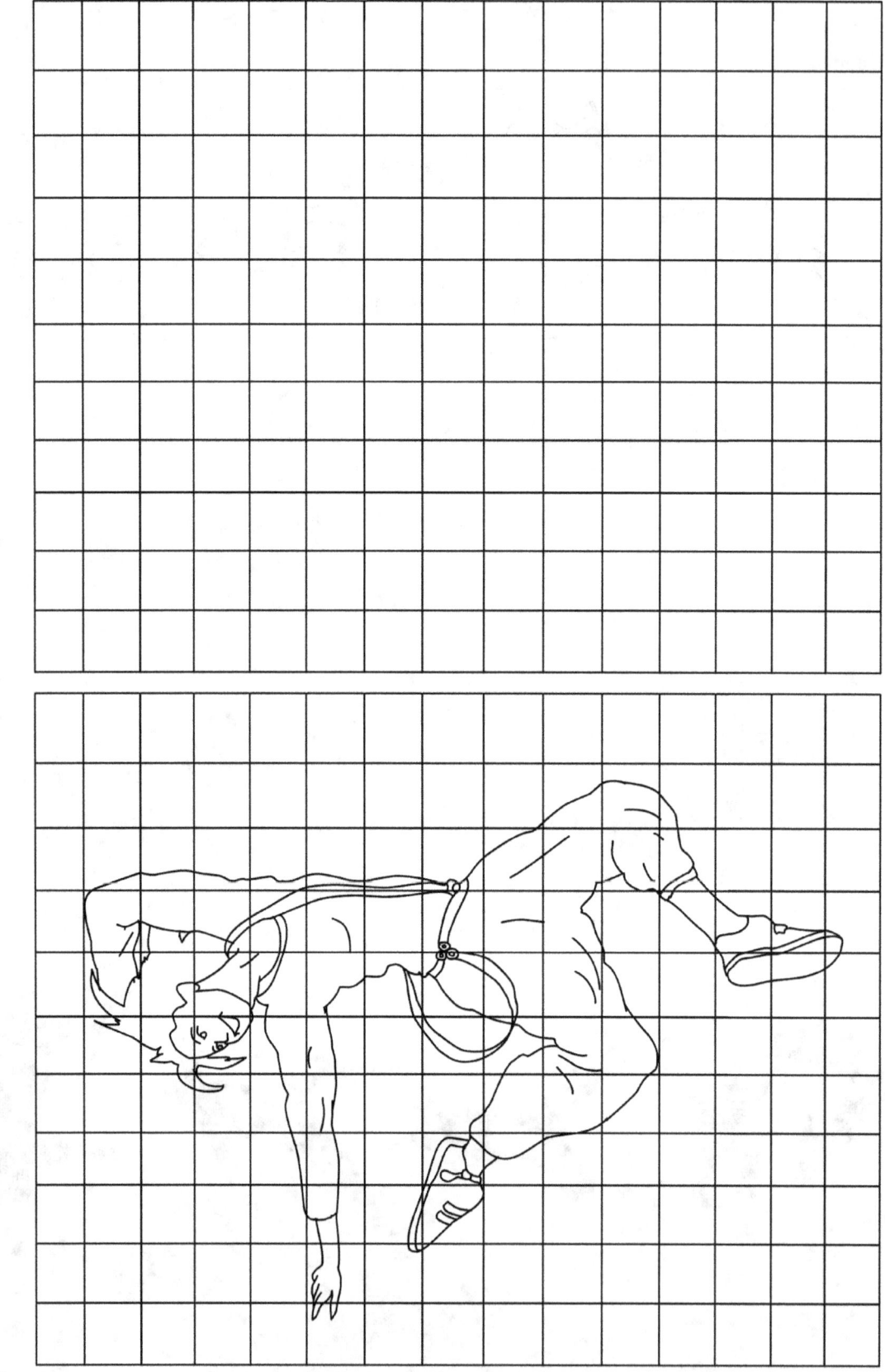

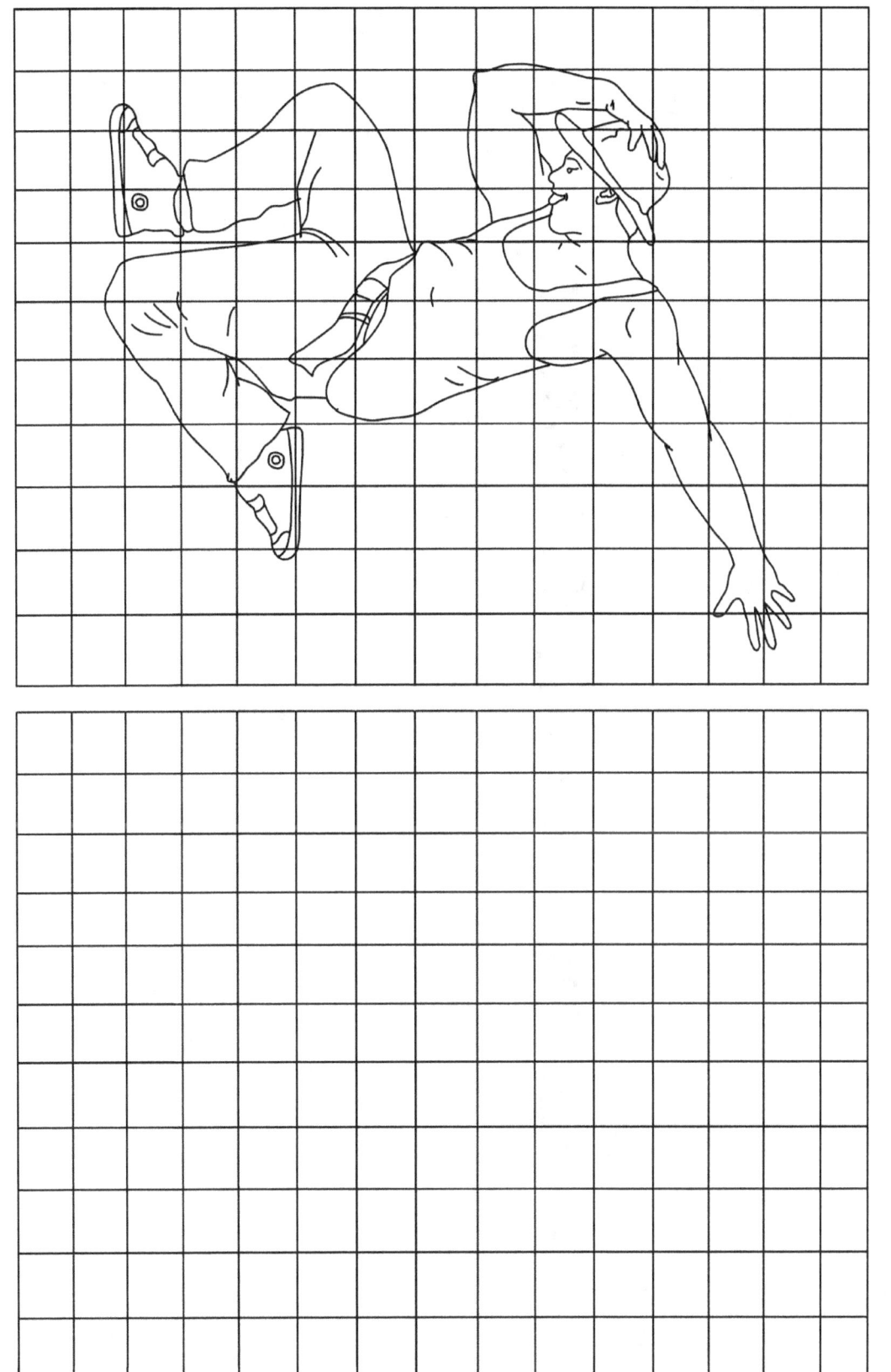

Copy the Picture

Copy the picture using the grid lines as a guide
you might find it easier to copy one square at a time

Intentionally Left Blank

1. cut and out all the parts
2. Arrange parts by order.

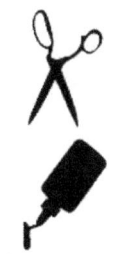

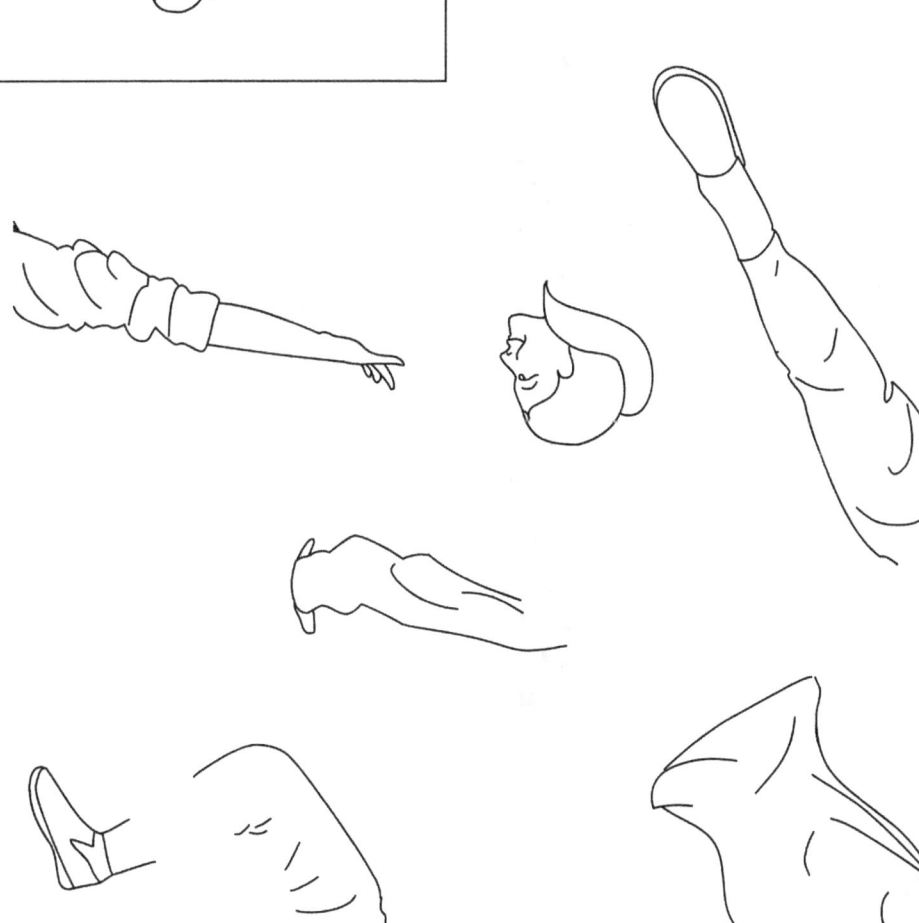

Intentionally Left Blank

1. cut and out all the parts
2. Arrange parts by order.

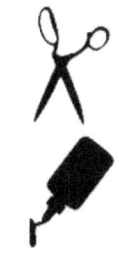

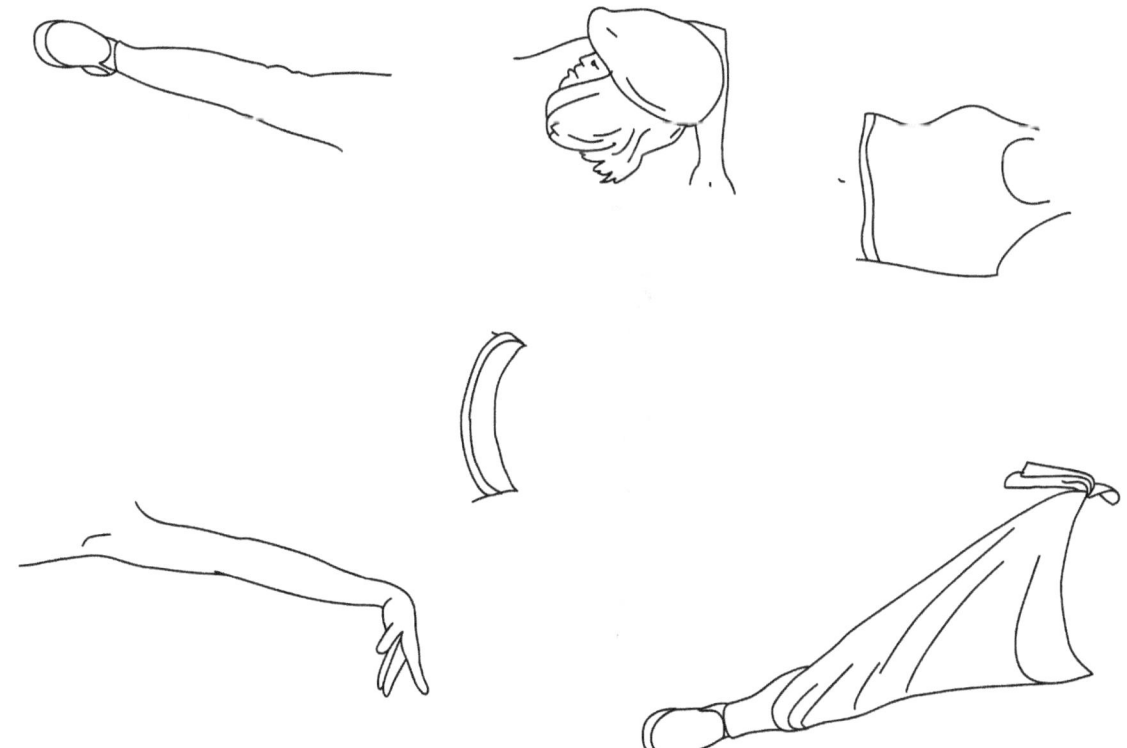

Intentionally Left Blank

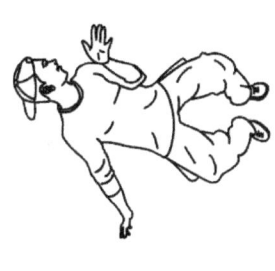
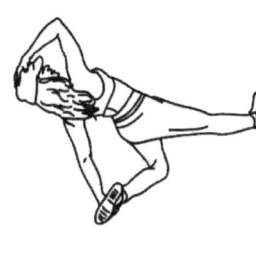
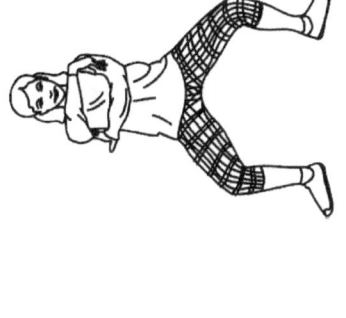

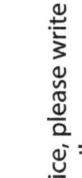
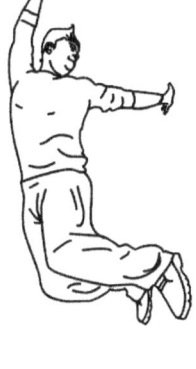
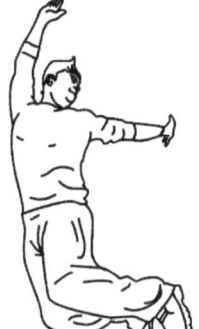

Hip Hop is a very personal dance. Truly, Hip Hop is an expression of one's personality and aspirations in life. It is about making something "totally you". This Dynamic Hip Hop Coloring and Activity Book is a part of my vision to inspire children to try out different body movements through dance, sport and other fields. It is and has been my life-long dream. I aspire for them to be exposed to physical activities so they will be able to enhance and express themselves better. And what better way to do it than by making them interested first? Coloring and activity books are the perfect platform to make them interested in things, so this is my personal way of reaching out to you. Each page is the product of countless daydreams and sleepless nights conceptualizing this coloring and activity book. The question has always been this, "What can inspire your children to love the dances and sports that I personally love?"

I hope you and your children will enjoy this book as much as I enjoyed making it. Thank you from the bottom of my heart,

Sincerely,
Idan Boaz

If you have any comments or advice, please write me:
info@idanboaz.co.il
www.ib-books.com

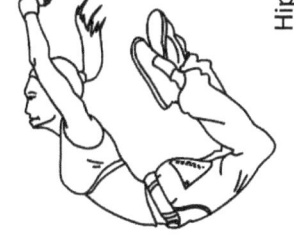
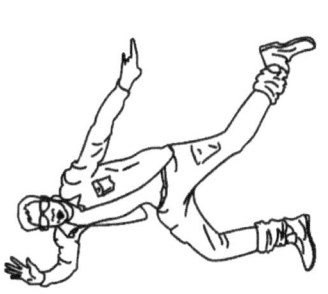

www.ingramcontent.com/pod-product-compliance
Lightning Source LLC
Chambersburg PA
CBHW081135180526
45170CB00008B/3112